I0815599

God's COLORFUL Easter

The Good News Is for Everyone

written by Esau McCaulley
illustrated by Rogério Coelho

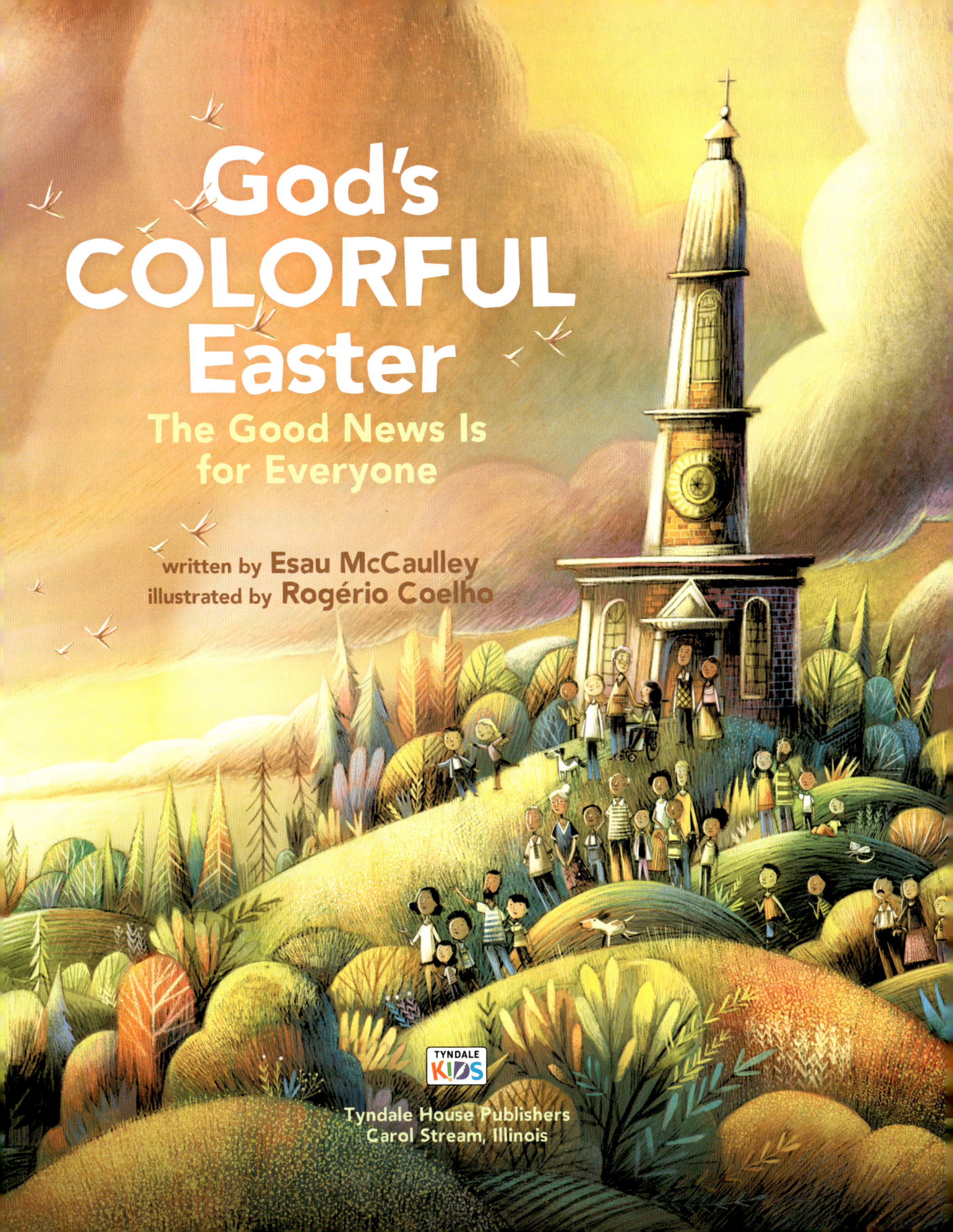

Tyndale House Publishers
Carol Stream, Illinois

Visit Tyndale's website for kids at tyndale.com/kids.

Visit the author's website at esaumccaulley.com.

God's Colorful Easter: The Good News Is for Everyone

Spot illustrations colorized by Olivia Jensen

Designed by Jacqueline L. Nuñez

For manufacturing information regarding this product, please call 1-855-277-9400.

For information about special discounts for bulk purchases, please contact Tyndale House Publishers at csresponse@tyndale.com, or call 1-855-277-9400.

Library of Congress Cataloging-in-Publication Data

A catalog record for this book is available from the Library of Congress.

ISBN 979-8-4005-0102-9

Printed in China

32 31 30 29 28 27 26

7 6 5 4 3 2 1

When we imagine heroes today, we think of swords and punches. Aren't heroes supposed to fight?

This book is about a different kind of hero. In fact, you're going to meet two heroes in our story. Neither one ever shot laser beams from his fingertips or swung a sword at dragons.

First, I want to introduce you to a man named Simon who played a small role in God's greatest miracle ever. Later in our story, you'll meet JESUS, THE GREATEST HERO OF ALL TIME.

Simon had traveled all the way from North Africa to Jerusalem. He and his family worshiped God there during the season of Passover, a holiday that celebrates God's great rescue of his people from slavery in Egypt. Simon must have wondered when God would do something that amazing again.

One day Simon saw a crowd of people following a man down the road as he carried a heavy wooden cross. Simon stopped a member of the crowd and asked, "Who is this? What is going on?"

"THIS IS JESUS OF NAZARETH—the one who performed all the miracles and claimed to be the Savior."

Simon saw Jesus, tired and bloody, and he felt sorry for this man. Then Simon made eye contact with a soldier, who yelled, "Come here!"

Simon went quickly.

The soldier said, "He is too weak to carry this cross. Help him!"

Simon did as he was told. As he lifted the cross, Simon must have thought, *There is something about this man. He is no common criminal.*

Simon walked with Jesus all the way up the hill, and then he slid back into the crowd, shaken by what had happened.

When Jesus died, it seemed like a defeat. But God is good at turning defeats into victories.

Jesus wasn't a hero who fought with fists or swords. Instead of fighting, JESUS HEALED. He died on the cross to show us how far God's love reaches.

Jesus took the punishment that we deserve and made it possible for us to turn toward God. By dying in our place, **JESUS DEFEATED THE POWER OF SIN AND DEATH** for everyone who chooses to follow him.

After Jesus died and was placed in a tomb, some of the women who followed him didn't know what to do. Then one of them had an idea: The least they could do was honor his body.

"Let's go to the tomb and pour oil and spices on Jesus' body," said Mary Magdalene.

"How will we get to him with that huge stone in front of the tomb?" another woman named Mary wondered.

"We'll cross that bridge when we come to it," said Mary Magdalene. "Let's go!"

When they arrived at the tomb, the ground beneath their feet started to shake. It was an earthquake!

Then something even more
terrifying took place. An angel
came down from heaven.
He was as bright as lightning.
The women's jaws dropped.

THE ANGEL ROLLED AWAY THE GIANT STONE. The guards at the tomb were so afraid they started trembling and fell to the ground.

The angel said to the women, "Do not be afraid, for I know that you are looking for Jesus, who was crucified. HE IS NOT HERE; HE HAS RISEN, just as he said. Come see the place where he lay."

The women saw the empty tomb and were amazed. They were bursting with happiness and excitement. They had to share the news with others! They ran back to tell Jesus' other disciples.

On their way, the women met Jesus.

"Don't be afraid!" he told them.

Later, Jesus met up with the rest of his disciples in Galilee.

The words of the angel were true! Jesus had risen from the dead.

If the death of Jesus was the world's saddest day, his resurrection was the day filled with the most joy. And this joy is not just for you and me. It is for the whole world.

God loves the whole world and wants everyone to know what Jesus, our Hero, has done. GOD WANTS ALL PEOPLE TO BELONG TO HIS COLORFUL KINGDOM.

Jesus spent forty days with his friends, and hundreds of people saw he was alive again. But Jesus had to return to be with God in heaven. Before he left, Jesus gave his followers an important job. He said, "Go and make disciples of all the different peoples of the world. Teach them all that I taught you."

That includes everything Jesus said about love, obedience, justice, and compassion.

"Baptize them in the name of the Father, the Son, and the Holy Spirit," Jesus said. "No matter what hap-pens, know that I AM WITH YOU. Even to the very end of the age."

We are Christians today because somebody listened to Jesus and brought the good news of his love to us and our family. There are Christians of every color, on every continent.

Remember Simon? He and his sons joined God's new family after JESUS–THE GREATEST HERO–rose from the dead. God always wanted a beautifully diverse family gathered around the cross. Simon was just one part of God's colorful Kingdom.

God's plan is unfolding.
HIS COLORFUL KINGDOM IS GROWING.
His work continues through us.

About the Author

Rev. Esau McCaulley, PhD, is associate professor of New Testament and the Jonathan Blanchard Chair of New Testament and Public Theology at Wheaton College in Wheaton, Illinois. Dr. McCaulley's research and writing focus is on New Testament exegesis, African American biblical interpretation, and public theology. He is the author of *How Far to the Promised Land: One Black Family's Story of Hope and Survival in the American South*, *Reading While Black: African American Biblical Interpretation as an Exercise in Hope*, *Josey Johnson's Hair and the Holy Spirit*, and *Andy Johnson and the March for Justice*. Dr. McCaulley is also a contributing opinion writer for *The New York Times*. His writings have appeared in *The Atlantic*, *The Washington Post*, and *Christianity Today*. He is married to Mandy, a pediatrician and Navy reservist. Together, they have four wonderful children.

About the Illustrator

Rogério Coelho lives in Curitiba, a city in the south of Brazil. He has worked as a professional illustrator for twenty-five years, illustrating more than one hundred books for Brazilian publishers, and has twice received the Jabuti Award (2012 and 2016), Brazil's most important literary award. In 2015, Rogério began illustrating for publishers in England (*Storytime Magazine*, a magazine aimed at children) and in the United States. His wordless picture book *Boat of Dreams* received starred reviews from *School Library Journal* and *Booklist*, was named a Best Book for Kids by the New York Public Library in 2017, and received the Independent Publisher Book Awards' gold medal for children's picture books. Rogério also illustrated *You Be You* (written by Richard Brehm), which received the same gold medal for children's picture books in 2021.